Understand and Break Free From Your Own Limitations

MATTHEW BRIGHTHOUSE

Copyright © 2017

Table of Contents

1 INTRODUCTION 3
2 THE FINE LINE BETWEEN STRENGTH AND WEAKNESS 7
3 ALLOW YOURSELF TO BE EMOTIONAL 14
4 LEARN TO GO WITH THE FLOW 17
5 CONCENTRATE ON YOUR ROMANTIC LIFE 20
6 LEARN TO BE LESS JUDGEMENTAL, BE HUMBLE 24
7 UNDERSTAND IT'S OKAY TO FAIL 27
8 LEARN TO ADMIT YOU CAN BE WRONG 31
9 CONCLUSION 35

1
Introduction

The fact you have picked up this book tells us that you have taken the Myers-Briggs Personality Test, and you have come out as an INTJ personality type. Obviously, being a curious person who is always looking to learn something new, you want to know what this is all about, and you want to know how you can use it and develop yourself further.

You might not know it yet, but this is a key trait of your INTJ personality type.

You are a rare breed, as just 2% of the overall population is thought to be this particular type – that makes you extra special! It is also thought that men are more likely to be an INTJ type, with less than 1% of the population a female INTJ type.

As an INTJ you are an introvert, a quiet person who is always thinking, always looking for a solution to a problem, and always taking in your surroundings. You are known as The Mastermind, and that is because you are likely to be highly intelligent, driven, and always striving for success. Failure is not an option for an INTJ, and as a result, you are likely to be someone who is either studying a highly intellectual subject, or you are high up in your business/job. An INTJ is constantly on the lookout for another success, and another intellectual goal.

So, what does INTJ stand for?

I = Introversion

N = Intuition

T = Thinking

J = Judgement

Let's check them out one by one.

- **Introversion** - You are, as we mentioned, an introvert, and that means that you are more likely to sit and take in your surroundings, listening and absorbing, than you are talking and being the life and soul of the job. This is a good thing for you because it helps you find new opportunities and creative solutions to problems, which would have otherwise gone unnoticed.

- **Intuition** – As an INTJ, you are likely to be highly intuitive, but not in an emotional way. Instead, an INTJ personality type focuses much more on logic and what makes factual sense. In order to grow personally, therefore, you should learn to trust your emotional instincts as well as your mind-related instincts, in order to find more emotional solutions to problems and to help you develop and grow in personal relationships.

- **Thinking** – An INTJ has a very powerful mind, so you are likely to be always thinking about something – you never stop! This can be tiring but it certainly helps you to find solutions to issues and it also helps you climb up that career ladder. As an INTJ, you are an ideal business person, and entrepreneur, and someone who is successful in most things you put your mind to.

- **Judgement** – Perhaps one of the downsides of being an INTJ is that you can be rather judgmental of others. Now, you don't mean this in a malicious way, instead, you can't understand why others don't think with the same 'go-getter' mindset that you do. What you need to remember however is that you are a rare type, so it's more probable that you will come into contact with people who aren't like you, compared to the number who think the same way.

The hope is that you are reading the description set and you are nodding along, recognizing parts of yourself in what you're reading. Of course, it could also be that you're not too sure because we don't often see the traits in ourselves that others do or the traits which come out in tests, such as the Myers-Briggs. As you go through this book, however, you will begin to see more and more how your INTJ personality type shapes the way you think and act, and by taking in the methods for self-improvement that we're going to talk about, you will be able to push yourself to further success in the future.

Success is highly important to an INTJ, as you will have read already, but that doesn't mean success in business per se. Success comes in many different forms, and this is something that you really need to open your eyes to as an INTJ. You love to succeed in business and in your job, and that's an admirable trait, for sure, but you could develop yourself further by recognizing that success in personal relationships is just as important.

We are going to talk in much more detail about this as we move through our chapters, but the important thing to remember is to keep an open mind. Of course, as an INTJ, that is something you're very good at already! You are one of the most open-minded of all the personality types, and that is another positive trait of yours.

Of course, not everyone is 100% in one particular personality type, and we all display traits of the other types from time to time. However, if you notice yourself displaying another type's traits a bit more often, it would do you good to read up about that particular type also and to incorporate self-development tricks related to that, into your INTJ development work. This will surely help you become a well-rounded individual, someone who is aware of their strengths and weaknesses, and who doesn't allow anything to hold them back.

So, you are a rare breed, an interesting breed; let's look into your strengths and your weaknesses, before going on to talk about how you can develop those weaknesses into major positives in your life.

2
The Fine Line Between Strength And Weakness

Every single one of us has a set of strengths and a set of weaknesses. This is a normal 'thing' about being human, and it is something we can't escape from. Having said that, what you can do is learn to turn those weaknesses into positives, by understanding them and learning to change your current way of thinking.

As an INTJ you are somewhat of an enigma. You are not someone who likes to fail at anything, but that is fine in many ways, as you don't fail that often anyway. When you do, however, it can feel like the end of the world, and it is something which can force you to feel down. What you would benefit from realizing, however, is that failing is not a negative, it is something to be learned from, in order to do better next time, and perhaps to teach you a lesson about the way you handled a situation.

An INTJ personality type is not really known as being the most friendly or sociable of creatures, and whilst you might be reading that and thinking 'how rude!', think about your past relationships for a second. Did you give yourself completely and emotionally to another person? Or, more likely, did you find it hard to let go, and instead kept a large amount of yourself back? An INTJ is not an emotional being, they push their emotions down, and if you are a true INTJ, you will notice this quite easily.

To really understand what we're talking about, let's check out the strengths and weaknesses of your personality type. This will help you truly identify the areas you need to focus your work on.

INTJ Personality Type Strengths

- **Highly intelligent** – INTJs are known for their strong and powerful minds, and are very good at thinking outside the box, strategically in particular. As this personality type, you will be someone who likes to learn, who takes every opportunity to find new and interesting subjects to learn about and absorb the knowledge. This, of course, means that you are in a greater position to use that knowledge to push yourself to further success in whatever field it pertains to, and this is a key personality trait of your type. You are also likely to have a very strategic way of thinking, i.e. you plan everything out and exclude the plan to perfection. If you fail to tick any box along the way, you can be incredibly hard on yourself. Basically, as an INTJ, your mind is like a sponge, ready to absorb any new knowledge you can.

- **Always love a challenge** – An INTJ is unlikely to turn down a challenge, and a little like a dog with a bone, they will not let go until it is finished to success! You are someone who is curious, and that means you are always looking for something new to push yourself, to learn from, and to use in the future when working to solve another problem or tick something else off your 'to do' list. You have a creative mind, but you don't use your creativity in an artsy way, instead, you use it in a strategic way to cover all aspects and all eventualities.

- **High self-esteem and self-confidence** – INTJs do not doubt themselves, and that is a major plus point in decision making. When you make a choice, you stick to it, and you always believe that you made the right decision, without swaying either way. You are not someone who thinks 'maybe I made a mistake', because you thought through it all completely before you made the decision, so you have no doubts in either direction. Basically, once you make up your mind, there's no changing it.

- **Very independent** – You are not someone who relies on anyone else to get on in life, and that is a very positive trait to have. You are not needy, and you are not 'soft', instead you can be relied upon to survive and succeed in any situation, and your highly decisive nature means that a decision, once made, is final.

- **Very hard working** – If you want a job done and done well, call an INTJ! You place high importance on your career because success reflects back on you as a person. For that reason, you work hard to get where you want to be, and you are determined, meaning that you don't stop until you get there. The downside of this is that an INTJ often doesn't know when to stop, so you are likely to be someone who is first in the office in the morning, and the last to leave at night!

- **Very open-minded** – You are not someone who is closed off to the world, and because you are always thinking outside the box and strategically making your way up the ladder, you are very open-minded and liberated. This relates to situations, people, and everything in-between. To you, a person is a person, and a situation is a situation, and you don't have a strong or swayed opinion on anything that isn't based on fact or logic.

As you can see, the positive INTJ personality traits are all success-focused. You are a go-getter, you are someone who loves to challenge themselves and gets a real kick out of success. You work hard to get where you want to be, and you are fiercely independent in the process. For a quality job done well, an INTJ is always the best person to call.

Now, because everything in life has a flip side, and because we want to help you develop and grow, let's check out the main weaknesses of an INTJ personality type.

INTJ Personality Weaknesses

The downside of being an INTJ personality type is main to do with the way you may come across to others, and the fact that you rarely recognize or use your emotions in your daily life. This can affect the way you develop relationships if you bother to do that at all, and it can mean that you become isolated and too work-focused.

Let's explore this a little more closely.

- **A tendency towards arrogance** – Because you are so factual, analytical and you push towards success at any cost (sometimes), this can mean that you come across to other people as quite arrogant. You don't understand people who don't try and challenge themselves and succeed, and those who are more emotionally-based can appear to be 'weak' to you. This is simply the way you think, and not the fact that you are literally arrogant, but you do need to be mindful of how you are displaying yourself to other people. If you come across as overly arrogant, you are unlikely to be someone who is surrounded by a large social circle, which is needed in life. Overall, an INTJ has few friends and sticks with the same close circle, usually other factually minded personality types.

- **You can be a little judgemental** – We just mentioned that as an INTJ you don't really understand people who don't try hard to succeed, and that can make you judgmental. You need to realize that everyone has different mindsets and that just because someone prefers to focus on their relationships or their emotions and home life, it doesn't mean that they are failing, and doesn't mean that they are in any way underachieving. Everyone's focus is different, and it is important to have an open mind about this, as open as you have about the other things in life. We did mention that you are generally quite open-minded as a personality type, but when it comes to being judgemental, you tend to contradict yourself somewhat.

- **You are over-analytical to a degree** – You simply don't know when to let it go! You are like a dog with a bone and until you see your task to the end, and succeed, you will not stop. This is a good thing to a degree, but it can lead you to exhaustion, and it can make you neglect the people in your life. You need some time for yourself too! INTJs don't tend to understand the concept of a home/work-life balance, and they tend to be much more leaning towards the work side of things. If you can learn to balance it out, whilst keeping your fantastic tenacity, you will be on a wonderful road towards success in many areas of your life.

- **You do not flourish well within structure** – There is a reason why so many INTJs are self-employed or work higher up the corporate ladder! As an INTJ you are likely to dislike any kind of formal structure because you find it too suffocating. You need the freedom to work and focus on where you need to go in your mind. It's not that you are particularly arrogant in terms of not wanting people around you to suffocate your analytical mind, but that you just can't stand the distraction. You place so much importance on success that anything which threatens to get in the way of it, is not something you tolerate well.

- **Your romantic relationships suffer** – Emotions, romantic relationships and friendships tend to take somewhat of a back-burner in your life as an INTJ. This isn't necessarily that you want it to be this way, you just don't give them the same level of attention as you do your work and strive for success. In order to achieve that balance we were talking about earlier, you need to open up your emotions and allow yourself to try and relate to others. This will enrich your life beyond measure and will actually give you the best of both worlds. Learning to feel, trust, and manage your emotions should be high up on your list of self-development topics.

If you're reading those weaknesses and wondering where to begin, don't worry! We are going to give you plenty of pointers in the coming chapters, that will help you address the above weaknesses, and achieve a greater balance in your life. As an INTJ, however, you may find a few of those weaknesses to be strange, or even unacceptable to you – this is part of your personality make up. What we are going to ask you to do, however, is to keep that mind open, as you are so good at doing. If you can open yourself up to accept and work on the following issues, you will be a truly well-rounded individual someone who can have those romantic relationships and fulfilling friendships, and still work so wonderfully well to achieve any success they put their mind to.

Consider this your greatest challenge, and we know that you love a challenge!

3
Allow Yourself to be Emotional

Dear INTJ, you are a truly logical and analytical soul. You trust facts, you trust your mind, you are totally forward-thinking, and you don't trust anything which doesn't make sense to your mind. For instance, you're not someone who is likely to be trusting fate and destiny, instead, you're going to trust science.

The problem with this is that you can easily turn off your emotions, and focus too much on your mind. Not everything in life makes sense, not everything has to add up to a logical solution. Whilst it is going to be hard for you to accept that you can trust a feeling, a hunch, it is something that you can learn to do over time.

Emotions are an important part of being a human being. We are born with feelings, and they develop as we grow. Some of us are more emotional than others, but it's important to allow your feelings to come to the fore and simply 'be'. You don't have to act on them, you don't have to particularly vocalize them, but you do need to recognize them as being valid.

The positive in allowing yourself to open up to feeling and emotions is that it will help you to click and develop friendships and relationships in the future – when you are ready. We are going to cover romantic relationships in more detail later on because it is such a huge part of being an INTJ. You don't flourish so well in romance, probably because it is a very emotional subject which requires compromise and sensitivity – not two traits which are particularly focused on your personality type! Do not worry though, and do not think that this in any way makes you a bad person, because it certainly doesn't. If you are hard-wired to think in one way, opening up to another way of thinking takes time and effort. If you can put in this time and effort then you will be able to have the best of the logical world and the emotional world.

How to Recognise and Open up to Your Emotions

Of course, it's not that you don't have any feelings, you don't have an 'off' switch, but you find it hard to deal with them because they don't make any logical sense to you. The next time you notice that you are feeling a certain way about a situation, e.g. perhaps angry or sad, simply acknowledge it first. Quietly sit and accept what you are feeling, put a title to it if you can; e.g. are you feeling rage? Are you feeling neglected? Are you feeling lonely? Are you feeling hurt? Are you feeling happy? Do you feel jealous? Perhaps you feel bored? Put a title to the way you are feeling.

Once you have acknowledged the feeling, you are halfway there. Basically, this means you are allowing yourself to feel, you are allowing yourself to feel validation in having that emotion in your life. Remember, just because there is no logical reason for feeling angry/jealous/happy/sad/lonely, whatever it is you're feeling, it doesn't mean it isn't real, and it doesn't mean it is weak or negative. Feeling is healthy, it allows you to deal with the situations in your life which are causing you distress, and it helps push you to reach new opportunities.

Now, once you know what you are feeling, and you have accepted it, allow yourself to explore it. What can you do about the way you are feeling? As an INTJ you love a challenge and you love to work something out, so use those positive traits to help you with this weakness. If you feel sad, what is making you feel sad, and what can you do to change that? If you are feeling jealous, why are you feeling that way? Are you thinking about the situation correctly? If you are happy, that's great! But, what part of your life is making you happy and when can you incorporate it into your time more often?

Becoming more used to recognizing and feeling your emotions is not about weakness, it's about simply accepting your feelings as a normal part of being human, and to realize that to feel is to be strong.

Meditation is another area which may help you become more at one with you who you are on the inside, and whilst as a logical INTJ you might totally roll your eyes at that suggestion, what's stopping you from trying it? Go on, we dare you!

4
Learn to go With The Flow

The problem with the flow, in the mind of an INTJ, is that it cannot be controlled, it doesn't have a set destination, and there is no way to really make sense of it.

As an INTJ, you are probably thinking that you need a plan, you need to challenge yourself to succeed, and the flow has no real direction that is useful to you. Now – stop right there!

The flow means that you are giving up control, you are putting trust in whatever will be. The thing you need to accept is that the flow is actually very beneficial to you and your future development. Someone who refuses to let go and see where life takes them can come across as rigid, too stuck, and untrusting in a process. You have a logical mind, and if the flow doesn't make actual sense then you won't do it.

For a second, however, perhaps try that flow out for size.

There is such a thing as 'what if', and many INTJs don't tend to subscribe to them. 'What if' is something which is very hard to live with and very hard to accept in the future. If you don't try, you don't know. Now, the 'what if' might not have had a logical answer to it at the time. Perhaps when you analyzed it, as you would have done, you didn't see a real point in pursuing the issue, or you didn't see how it could ever work out. But, what if you didn't see a small part of the road? What if there was something you missed? The flow would have brought that to the surface, but if you simply refuse to follow that flow, you will miss it and never know.

Does that make sense to you?

Logically isn't always the way forward, just like not giving any thought to thing isn't the way forward either. There is a balance that has to be found, and when it comes to following the flow, you need to analyze to a degree and make your decision, but also you need to think about the 'what if' too. If that 'what if' is something that niggles away at you, something which your intuition says is worth a shot, then go with that flow and don't try and control it.

The flow doesn't need to be controlled, otherwise, it won't be the flow!

Life is full of twists and turns, and this is something which an INTJ needs to recognize. You cannot control life because it doesn't make logical sense; very few things in life do, but does that mean they should be missed out on because there was no analytical sense to them? No!

For instance, if you are a soccer fan, you probably heard of David Beckham.

Now, David Beckham didn't grow up in a blessed household, he didn't come from money, but he loved his soccer. Now, moving to Manchester to join a football academy at a young age probably didn't make any analytical sense, in fact, it was a huge risk that could have backfired massively. Did he listen to the analytical side of his mind? No. He took the chance because the flow could have taken him somewhere, and it worked out massively.

If Mr. Beckham hadn't entertained said flow, he would probably not be the huge superstar he is now, he wouldn't be helping millions of people across the world through his various charity work and he wouldn't have met Victoria!

That is just one example, and you're probably reading it and thinking that it's a story of chance, but it wasn't – it was a story of hard work and careful planning. The flow doesn't have to be about totally letting go, it can simply be about losing the reigns a little. As a careful INTJ, if you allow your grip on those reigns to be a little less, you can open up your world to new chances and possible new opportunities.

5
Concentrate on Your Romantic Life

You might have noticed that up to now, all our development chapters have been about getting in touch with the way you're feeling, refusing to bow to logic totally and to let go a little. That's no mistake because the biggest downfall of an INTJ is about becoming too challenge and task focused, and pushing away any outside influence.

This particular chapter may not be pertinent to you, because there are many INTJ types who are settled down, married, cohabiting, and basically enjoying their relationship with their significant other, but there are also many others who aren't. The reason for this isn't about not meeting the right person per se, it's about not *being* the right person.

By reading this book so far, you will know that an INTJ doesn't tend to put much importance towards emotions, and places more on the mind. You can't love someone with your mind, you have to open your heart and feel it in your chest. This isn't to say that an INTJ is totally incapable of love, far from it! What we are saying is that you rare INTJs out there are more likely to push potential relationships away because they are too busy focusing on work, challenges, and succeeding.

What you have to remember is that a title, medal, award, or success is not going to keep you warm when you are old and grey, and one of your greatest successes in life should be about finding the person with whom you connect and grow with – together.

This chapter is about focusing on your romantic life a little more, but this doesn't mean you need to take time away from your work or studies and instead join a dating site – it's about finding ways to open yourself up to put more importance on the subject. Here are a few ideas how:

- Give yourself a night off! – Allow yourself social time, away from work or challenge in your mind
- Arrange a night out with people from work, those who are in the same line of work as you, and can understand your drive and determination
- Become more aware of your emotions and validate them
- Think carefully about your future, do you want to have someone by your side in the future?

Now, the problem you will have an INTJ is that you have a tendency to come across as cold, and that isn't because you necessarily are, but it is because you don't understand the things which aren't logical. As we mentioned in our previous chapter, being able to understand and own your emotions is key. You cannot form a relationship or bond with someone if you cannot dedicate the time to them – nobody is going to stick around if they feel second best or neglected. Now, again, this isn't your personal fault it is just your way of thinking, but it is something which needs to change.

Work is important of course, and challenges on bettering yourself should always be up there, but relationships and love are vital in happy lives. A home/work balance is something we have mentioned you may have trouble managing, but if you can ensure you dedicate the time to your partner, you will be able to forge a happy and successful relationships – and as an INTJ, you love success!

Love Doesn't have a Pre-Determined Outcome

An INTJ assesses everything in life to find out whether there is a chance of success or not. A relationship cannot be looked at this way! You are likely to see a potential partner as a project at first, perhaps assessing whether the modicum amount of risk is worth it and whether this person is going to bring you what you need to succeed, e.g. the outcome you want, perhaps a longer-term relationship, marriage children, or another outcome that is success to you.

This particular area, therefore, links in really well with our subject of going with the flow. If you are going to trust the flow of anything in life, it has to be in relationships of a romantic nature. There is no set outcome to any relationship, things happen and our feelings can change like the wind, but the point is that you have to go with it, to find out what happens. Think of it as a soap opera or a movie that you want to see the end of!

Open up, be brave, consider the other person, go with the flow, and avoid over-analytical thoughts.

6
Learn to Be Less Judgemental, Be Humble

One of the key weaknesses of an INTJ personality type is the tendency to be judgemental. Anyone who isn't focused, who doesn't strive for success, or doesn't make any basic sense to this type of personality, simply won't be tolerated, and judgment will set in.

Allowing yourself to recognize that everyone is different, and not everyone is so focused on success, is a key to self-development in your particular personality type. Let everyone do what they want to do, you can only control yourself, you can only tell yourself how to feel, and you can only do your own thing, and let it rise or fall.

What Does It Mean to Be Humble?

Learning to become more in touch with your emotions will allow you to become a more humble type of human being. This is about empathy, but it's also about letting the small things go. We are all different, we all have different aims, we all have different focuses in life. You don't know the story of someone else, you don't know what battles they are fighting behind the scenes, and you don't know why they feel certain things in life are important to them. Developing a humble outlook means you are developing yourself as a human being, and it will certainly help you to open yourself up to your own emotions.

You can learn a lot from other people and their lives, and we know that as an INTJ you love to learn! See other people as a learning experience and you will find it much easier to understand life from a different standpoint.

Being humble is to be tolerant, and tolerance has its roots in open-mindedness. We know that an INTJ is quite open-minded because you think through so many different options to solve an issue or to form an approach. Your analytical mind is very open to differences, but that can go either way – you can either be tolerant and humble, appreciative of your successes and gains, whilst being accepting of others', or you can go down the route of judgement, and instead focus on yourself and judge others for what you perceive to be failure.

We are going to talk about why it is okay to fail shortly, but you need to understand that not everyone's idea of failure is going to be your idea. Whilst you may see success as being the CEO of a business, someone else might see success as being happy in their job. Having the foresight to recognize this, and not to judge someone else's choices as failure is key to becoming a happier, more open, and generally more well-rounded individual.

Basically, we should celebrate each other's differences, and know that we all have a role to play in life. You may be the one who reaches the CEO position, but you need assistant's to keep you there, and you need administrative staff to keep the cogs turning – nobody's idea of success is better or worse than anyone else's. Judgement has no place in your life, and this is something you need to manage and begin to recognize.

7
Understand It's Okay to Fail

Don't be so hard on yourself!

As an INTJ, you want to do well, you want to be the best you can be, and you don't stop until you get there. But, what if the flow (that thing you need to follow occasionally), doesn't bring you the rewards you want? You need to understand that you cannot control everything in life, and sometimes it's just not meant to be. Yes, as an INTJ you struggle with such motions, but it's a truth.

Let's give you another celebrity example here – Simon Cowell. TV personality, business mogul, and generally very successful man. Did you know that Mr. Cowell was once bankrupt? Did that stop him from picking himself back up and focusing on his success once more? No! He took a chance and he didn't stop believing. If there is an individual to show you that it's okay to make mistakes, it's okay to fail occasionally, then it is Mr. Cowell himself.

The thing is, failure isn't always a failure, it's basically your own idea of failure. What you perceive as failure could be someone else's idea of success. Only by understanding that life does indeed work in mysterious ways occasionally can you really come to the point in your life where you have that famed balance of work and happiness.

What do You Class as Failure?

It's no good saying that this particular situation is a win and this particular one is a failure because as we just mentioned, everyone has a different idea of a win and a loss. You need to be clear in your mind what you want in life, of course, and you should do everything you can to get there but if you encounter a bump in the road, it's vital not to see it as a loss, and it's certainly important not to let that get you down and allow yourself to start dragging down that famed self-confidence of yours.

The ironic thing is that a 'failure' is a real opportunity for learning, and we know that as an INTJ you love to learn. Take the experience and soak up the knowledge to make the next time even better.

We know that as an INTJ you are extremely determined and confident, but even the most confident people in life stumble occasionally. The ironic thing is that these stumbles can often help us find something better in life because it changes our course. The course you were on perhaps wasn't going to bring you the successes that you wanted, but the new one could bring you something even better. It's really about taking every opportunity and working with it to see where it goes – if it doesn't work out, see it simply as a corner you need to turn, rather than a full stop. Life is a long and very winding road, to coin a phrase, and the end doesn't come until your days are done. No full stop and no failure.

Now, we have titled this chapter that it's okay to fail, but we have just said there really is no failure in life. That's not a contradiction by any means because it's really more about the way you think of situations in your mind. An INTJ is always going to think of anything other than total success as a failure. But, what is success? Again, you need to have a clear picture in your mind of what success is to you personally.

Readdressing your idea of failure is key to becoming much happier and calmer as an INTJ personality type.

What to do if You Really do 'Fail'

If you feel that you really didn't do the best you could do if you really do find yourself in a situation where you totally class it as a failure, how do you deal with it?

As an INTJ you are likely to struggle with this because you are hard-wired to doggedly pursue success at all costs. You will work tirelessly, determinedly, single-mindedly, but the truth of life is that sometimes it just won't work out, and there may be no actual solid reason for this. How do you deal with it?

Again, give yourself a break!

You are a determined person, so you're going to pick yourself back up, that's for sure, but there is some evidence to suggest that INTJ personality types are a little more susceptible to becoming down or even depressed because they expect so much from themselves. The bottom line is that you are human! You also don't allow yourself to feel your emotions as much as some other personality types, and that can in itself force you to feel like you have failed. Emotions are not a sign of weakness, and in order to be healthy on the inside and the outside, you need to address any issues which do arise if you are feeling low.

So, what do you do if you think you've failed? Basically, you pick yourself up, you dust yourself off, and you put your experience towards making sure you succeed the next time. It's really that simple. Use it as a mantra if you must, but remember this – it's really okay to 'fail' sometimes!

8
Learn to Admit You Can be Wrong

This is going to sound a little harsh, but it has to be said – you are not right all of the time!

As an INTJ you have a tendency to think that your way is the right way and that the way of others is either wrong or half-hearted. This is your judgemental side coming out! Now, remember that an INTJ is actually very open-minded, so this really does bring up a total contradiction once again!

Let's address something here, however – thinking that you are right and that others are wrong is nothing to do with their personal lives, religion or anything connected to it, because as an INTJ you are totally open-minded in that respect, we are actually talking about thinking you are right in the work you are doing, the challenge you are perusing. Basically, for a different personality type, working in a team with an INTJ can be a difficult situation, to say the least!

Your way is not the only way, and you need to open your mind to understand that perhaps the ideas of others could be a better option than your own – shock horror! We've mentioned it countless times, but INTJs love to learn, so turn your way of thinking around and understand that listening to others is about being mindful, but it is also about learning from other people and appreciating their input. Soak up those ideas and see what you can take from them.

Be Mindful of How You Come Across to Others

An INTJ is an introverted person, but you are far from shy, instead, you are a listener, a thinker, and someone who soaks up knowledge like a very absorbable sponge! Despite these admirable traits, you need to be a little mindful of how that could come across to other people. You tend to be so wrapped up in your own mind that you can shut out the world, including other people. This can lead them to think you are perhaps a little unsociable, and they could take an instant dislike to you.

This is perhaps doing a disserve to you because it doesn't mean you are a bad person by any means. If you can learn to open up a little and be a bit more mindful of how others may perceive you, then they will see that you are a wonderful person in your own right.

The biggest challenge for an INTJ personality is really about not only opening up emotionally, but it is also about forging relationships with others, either friendships, romantic relationships or working relationships. Other people can be easily put off by someone who comes across as 'thorny', whether they truly are that way inside or not. Our first impression of someone is extremely powerful, and this is something you need to bear in mind when meeting new people.

An INTJ Personality in a Team

When working in a team you also need to use that open-minded positivity to really listen to what people are saying. Other people do have great contributions to make, and if you listen to them, you could find a really useful piece of information in there, which you could use to help you work towards your own successes.

Patience, empathy, listening skills, and having respect for the views of others is something you do need to work as an INTJ personality. Again, that might sound harsh, but it's really about the way others perceive you, rather than your own shortcomings.

Introverts overall are great listeners, and with your enquiring mind, listening and soaking up information isn't difficult. What you need to work on is what you do with that information. Don't cast it aside simply because at face value it seems odd or illogical to you, and instead, try and think outside the box a little. Use that analytical mind of yours to think carefully about what they are saying, and to come up with creative ideas from that. If you can work together, using the other person's idea, and your logical and analytical take on it, you are really working together to make a team effort. We also know that teams are more likely to succeed than individuals, and with your total determination, success is your number one goal.

Be aware that perhaps you aren't the easiest person to work with as part of a team, and be mindful of your approach to the ideas of others. If you can do this, then you will certainly be a great team player and someone who others will look to for guidance and ideas.

9
Conclusion

So, there it is, you now know everything you need to know about your own INTJ personality, or perhaps, the personality of someone close to you. Reading the type of personality regarding someone you live with or you are close to, can actually be really useful in helping to understand them, so if it's not about you, you can take the information we've given you and use it to form a really well-researched opinion.

So, let's recap.

We know that an INTJ personality's main focus and areas are:

- Introvert
- Intuition
- Thinking
- Judgement

Those are both positives and they are also negatives because they can work in each camp.

As an INTJ you are a rare personality type, and we have said that only 2% of the general population comes up as a true INTJ. You might notice certain traits within this type that you display yourself and in that case, you should read the book over and take information and advice wherever you can, even if you're not a 100% in the INTJ camp. The fact this type of personality is rare really does tell you a lot about their focus and drive to succeed.

Some of the most successful people in the world are likely to have INTJ traits at the very least, and their dogged determination and will to succeed is what really pushes them forward. Of course, every personality type has weaknesses and downsides, but you can work with those negatives to make them into positives, or at least improve their impact significantly. An INTJ has problems with emotions and judgment, but we've been through some very useful advice and guidance on how to flip that around.

As an INTJ, you will probably never be someone who learns to live life by the seat of their pants, trusting in fate and destiny and being truly at one with your emotions, but you can learn to manage them, recognise them, and use them for good, rather than allow them to rule the negative sides of your personality.

One of the areas of your life where you will need to focus attention is your social and romantic side. You aren't the most romantic person on the planet, but that doesn't mean that you don't want to be loved and that you don't want this in your life. It's more about the act that you place more importance on other areas of your life, and perhaps by the time you realize this it could be that you've passed up a few opportunities already. It's never too late however, it's really about making the chance and recognizing that having a balance between success in your work life or in general areas is equal in importance to romance and relationships. You can't live alone all your life and be happy, and you can't snuggle up to spreadsheets and brainstorming charts at night! Everyone needs a balance, and this is something you need to work towards achieving.

Of course, you are a thinker, and you are someone who will think the life out something before giving up on it if you ever give up at all. You are determined and you are extremely hard working, and for that, you could congratulate yourself. A worker is an attractive trait, but remember that all work and no play does not make for a happy individual either! Again, it's down to balance.

Making The Most of Your Personality Type

Whether you are totally INTJ, or you simply display traits, you should definitely work to maximise the up points of your type. We focus a lot on the weaknesses, mainly because we want to help you turn them into positives, or manage them better; having said that, it's important to celebrate the positive sides of your type, and as we just mentioned, as an INTJ, you are someone who is always going to do well in life.

Don't read this book and be down about the negative points we've raised, because the point is you can take this information and learn from it, which is something you love to do. You aren't a bad person because you have a tendency to judge, but it's important to recognize our lesser points, so we can turn them into positives, and be mindful of how we perhaps come across to other people, whilst we are so caught up in the brilliance of our own minds.

We know that as an INTJ you are not someone who is amongst the higher percentages of the population, and as a rare personality type, you are really one of a kind. Celebrate that fact! This is something to be proud of, and if you can make the downsides up, then you have succeeded in perhaps the biggest challenge of your life. Changing the way you think and act due to your own traits isn't the easiest thing in the world, but hang on in there, because it can be done with plentiful time and effort.

An introvert will always be someone who flies below the radar, rather than above it, but if you can use that quiet confidence, whilst being mindful of everything else in your life, then your future is certainly shining golden, and as an INTJ, your future success is basically there for the taking anyway!

Note from the author

Thank you for purchasing and reading this book. If you enjoyed it or found it useful then I'd really appreciate it if you would post a short review on Amazon. I do read all the reviews personally so that I can continually write what people are wanting.
If you'd like to leave a review then please visit the link below:
https://www.amazon.com/dp/B07651LPP7
Thanks for your support and good luck!

Check Out My Other Books

Below you'll find some of my other books that are popular on Amazon and Kindle as well. Simply search the titles listed below on Amazon. Alternatively, you can visit my author page on Amazon to see other work done by me.

ENFP: Understand and Break Free From Your Own Limitations

INFP: Understand and Break Free From Your Own Limitations

ENFJ: Understand and Break Free From Your Own Limitations

INFJ: Understand and Break Free From Your Own Limitations

ENFP: INFP: ENFJ: INFJ: Understand and Break Free From Your Own Limitations – The Diplomat Bundle Series

INTP: Understand and Break Free From Your Own Limitations

OPTION B: F**K IT - How to Finally Take Control Of Your Life And Break Free From All Expectations. Live A Limitless, Fearless, Purpose Driven Life With Ultimate Freedom

Printed in Great Britain
by Amazon